WILEY **CPA** Examination Review

2nd Edition
Focus Notes

Accounting and Reporting

Mark Edward

JOHN WILEY & SONS, INC.

New York • Chichester • Weinheim • Brisbane • Singapore • Toronto

ISBN 0-471-38962-5

Printed in the United States of America

10 9 8 7 6 5 4 3 2 1

Contents

Preface

This publication is a comprehensive, yet simplified study program. It provides a review of all the basic skills and concepts tested on the CPA exam and teaches important strategies to take the exam faster and more accurately. This tool allows you to take control of the CPA exam.

This simplified and focused approach to studying for the CPA exam can be used:

- As a handy and convenient reference manual
- To solve exam questions
- To reinforce material being studied

Included is all of the information necessary to obtain a passing score on the CPA exam in a concise and easy-to-use format. Due to the wide variety of information covered on the exam, a number of techniques are included:

- Acronyms and mnemonics to help candidates learn and remember a variety of rules and checklists

- Formulas and equations that simplify complex calculations required on the exam

- Simplified outlines of key concepts without the details that encumber or distract from learning the essential elements

- Techniques that can be applied to problem solving or essay writing, such as preparing a multiple-step income statement, determining who will prevail in a legal conflict, or developing an audit program

- Pro forma statements, reports, and schedules that make it easy to prepare these items by simply filling in the blanks

- Proven techniques to help you become a smarter, sharper, and more accurate test taker

This publication may also be useful to university students enrolled in Intermediate, Advanced and Cost Accounting, Auditing, Business Law, and Federal Income Tax classes.

Good Luck on the Exam,
Mark Edward

About the Author

Mark Edward has been preparing individuals for the CPA exam since 1971. For many years, he taught CPA review classes for various universities, including the California State University at Northridge and the University of California at Los Angeles. He currently operates the largest CPA review program in the state of California, under the name *Mark's CPA Review Course,* with corporate offices located in Culver City California.

Mark Edward serves on the board of directors for the California Society of CPAs, and is a member or officer of the Institute of Management Accountants, the American Society of Women Accountants, the National Association of Black Accountants, the American Association of Hispanic CPAs and the Association of Governmental Accountants.

Corporate Income Tax

Corporate Formation

Services for Stock

Taxable transaction

- Taxable wages to stockholder = FMV of stock

- Stockholder basis in stock = FMV

- Corporation deducts wage expense = FMV of stock

Assets for Stock

Nontaxable transaction:

- Shareholders ownership ≥ 80%
- Shareholder basis in stock = basis in asset given (**carryover basis**)
- Corporation basis in asset = stockholder's basis

Taxable transaction

- Shareholder ownership < 80%
- Stockholder recognizes gain = FMV − basis
- Stockholder basis in stock = FMV
- Corporation basis in asset = FMV

Computing Corporate Income Tax

	Gross income
-	Deductions
=	Taxable income
X	Tax rate
=	Preliminary tax liability
+	Personal holding company tax
+	Accumulated earnings tax
+	Alternative minimum tax
=	Total tax liability
-	Credits
=	Net tax liability
-	Estimated payments
=	Tax due

Gross Income

Includes:

- Revenues

- Interest earned

- Dividends received

- Capital gains

- Other income

Excludes nontaxable items such as interest on municipal bonds

Deductions

Deductible expenses include:

- Ordinary & reasonable operating expenses
- Compensation costs including wages & bonuses
- Employer payroll taxes
- Fringe benefits including health & life insurance when employee selects beneficiary
- Interest on business indebtedness
- Bad debts when written off
- Meals & entertainment X 50%
- Straight line amortization of goodwill over 15 years
- Straight-line amortization of organization costs over at least 5 years

Deductions (continued)

Nondeductible expenses include:

- Fines, penalties, & punitive damages

- Compensation in excess of $1,000,000 paid to each of 5 highest paid executives

- Accrued compensation not paid within 2 ½ months after year end

- Interest expense on debt used to acquire nontaxable investments

- Premiums on key person insurance with company as beneficiary

- Club dues

- Cost of issuing, printing, & selling stock

Dividends-Received Deduction

1) Determine % for deduction

- Corporation's ownership < 20% - Deduct 70%

- Ownership ≥ 20% & < 80% - Deduct 80%

- Ownership ≥ 80% - Deduct 100%

2) Apply % to dividends or taxable income before deduction, whichever is lower

3) Exception – If % X dividends > taxable income, use entire amount, resulting in loss

Does not apply to:

- Dividends from a foreign corporation

- Dividends from a tax exempt organization

- Dividends on an investment held for less than 45 days

- Dividends from an investment acquired with borrowed funds

Personal Holding Company (PHC) Tax

Corporations subject to PHC tax if 2 conditions apply:

1) Interest, dividends, rents, royalties, or personal service contracts > 60% of gross income

2) 5 or fewer stockholders > 50% of total ownership

PHC tax

- Self assessed, along with regular return

- Amount = 39.6% X undistributed taxable income

- Added to regular tax

- Can be reduced by actual or consent dividends

Accumulated Earnings Tax

The accumulated earnings tax is not self assessed

- Not assessed to company paying PHC tax

- Assessed on earnings accumulated in excess of working capital or expansion needs

- Can be reduced by actual or consent dividends

Consent dividends – Shareholders pay personal income tax on dividends not actually declared or paid

Alternative Minimum Tax (AMT)

	Taxable income
±	Adjustments & preferences
=	Alternative minimum taxable income (AMTI)
−	Exemption
=	Base
X	Tax rate
=	Tentative minimum tax
−	Regular tax liability
=	AMT

Alternative Minimum Tax (continued)

Adjustments & preferences are added back to or deducted from taxable income in computing AMTI. They include:

- Interest on private activity municipal bonds

- Difference between depreciation for tax purposes and amount allowed for AMT purposes

- Adjusted current earnings (ACE) adjustment

Alternative Minimum Tax (continued)

ACE = the corporation's economic earnings

Taxable income

+   Nontaxable revenues

-      Nondeductible expenses

±   Nonfinancial revenues or expenses

=   ACE

Adjustments to taxable income in computing ACE generally include:

- **S**eventy percent dividends received deduction
- Life **I**nsurance proceeds
- **M**unicipal bond interest

> *There's a **slim** chance that you'll avoid the AMT.*

ACE adjustment = 75% X (ACE-AMTI)

Alternative Minimum Tax (continued)

AMTI is reduced by the **exemption** amount

Exemption = $40,000 − 25% X (AMTI - $150,000)

Resulting base amount X 20% = tentative minimum tax

Tentative minimum tax − regular income tax = AMT adjustment

- If tentative minimum tax > regular income tax − difference increases tax amount

- AMT paid in current year may be carried forward as credit to reduce regular taxes in future years

Foreign Tax Credit

Reduces income tax for taxes paid to foreign jurisdictions

Credit = smaller of

- Amount of foreign tax paid
- Foreign income ÷ total income X total tax liability

Supplemental Tax Schedules

Corporations include 2 supplemental schedules on their tax returns:

- **Schedule M-1** reconciles book income to taxable income

- **Schedule M-2** reconciles beginning retained earnings to ending retained earnings

Distributions to Stockholders

Cash Distributions

Treated as dividends when paid from earnings & profits (E &P)

- Can be paid out of current E & P, even if accumulated E & P is negative amount
- Can be paid out of accumulated E & P, even if current E & P is negative amount to extent accumulated E & P exceeds current E & P deficit

Dividends in excess of E & P:

- Not taxed as dividends
- Reduce shareholder tax basis in stock

Property Distributions

When property is distributed:

- Corporation recognizes gain if FMV > basis
- Corporation does not recognize loss if FMV < basis
- Shareholder recognizes dividend equal to FMV of property – loans assumed

Corporate Termination

Distributions of assets upon termination are liquidating distributions

- Corporation recognizes gain or loss when FMV ≠ basis in assets distributed
- Shareholder recognized capital gain or loss when FMV ≠ basis in stock

Upon termination of a subsidiary:

- Subsidiary recognizes no gains or losses on distributions of assets to parent
- Parent recognizes no gains or losses
- Parent's basis in assets = subsidiary's basis (**carryover basis**)

Corporate Reorganizations

Mergers & Acquisitions

Two or more companies form one company

When shareholders receive stock in new company for shares in old company

- No gain or loss recognized except to extent of cash received
- Carryover basis − basis in new shares = basis in old shares

Split-offs

One company divides into 2 or more separate entities

Parent-Subsidiary Transactions

Parent-subsidiary relationship exists when one company owns 80% or more of every class of another company's outstanding stock

- Companies may file consolidated return
- Intercompany transactions eliminated

Section 1244 Stock

Treatment as section 1244 stock applies if 2 conditions are met:

- Stock was issued as part of 1st $1,000,000 in capital raised by company
- Stock sold by original investor

Sales of section 1244 stock:

- Gains treated as capital gains
- Losses treated as ordinary to maximum of $50,000 per year

Depreciation

Depreciable Real Property

Depreciable real property is **section 1250** property, subject to the following rules

Useful Life

Useful life = 27.5 years for residential real property
Useful life = 39 years for other business real property

Depreciation Method

Depreciation calculated under straight-line

Mid-Month Convention

Year of purchase & year of sale

- Assumed purchased or sold in middle of month of transaction
- ½ month's depreciation taken regardless of date of transaction

Depreciable Personal Property

Depreciable personal property is section 1245 property, subject to the following rules

Section 179 Deduction

The section 179 deduction is a deduction

- Equal to cost of depreciable personal property acquired during year
- Deductible up to lower of net business earnings or a certain amount ($20,000 in 2000, $24,000 in 2001 & 2002, $25,000 in 2003 and after)
- Reduced by cost of property acquired in excess of $200,000 during year
- Amount deducted reduces depreciable basis of assets

Useful Life

Useful life is determined by nature of asset

- Equipment – 7 years
- Cars, light trucks, & computers – 5 years
- Small tools – 3 years

Depreciable Personal Property (continued)

Depreciation Method

The taxpayer may use either of 2 methods

- Straight-line
- Double-declining balance with a switch to straight-line in latter years of asset's life

Half-Year Convention

Generally required

- Assumes assets acquired or sold in middle of tax year
- ½ year's depreciation taken in year of acquisition & in year of sale

Mid-Quarter Convention

Must be applied in certain circumstances

- Applied when 40% or more of assets acquired in last 3 months of year
- Assumes assets acquired or sold in middle of quarter in which transaction occurs

Individual Income Tax

Computing Individual Income Tax

	Gross income
-	<u>Adjustments</u>
=	Adjusted gross income (AGI)
-	Standard deduction or itemized deductions
-	<u>Exemptions</u>
=	Taxable income
X	Tax rate
=	Tentative tax amount
-	Credits
+	Self-employment tax
+	Alternative minimum tax
=	Total tax
-	<u>Prepayments</u>
=	Tax due or refund amount

Accounting Method

Individuals apply the **cash basis** – Not allowed for
- Accounting for purchase & sales of inventory
- C corporations or partnerships with a C corporation partner
- Tax shelters
- Business with average gross receipts > $5,000,000

Income is reported when:
- Cash is received
- Property is received
- Taxpayer receives an unrestricted right to cash or property

Deductions are reported when:
- Cash is paid
- A check is disbursed
- An expense is charged to a credit card

Gross Income

Compensation for Services

Included:

- Wages, salaries, & tips
- Bonuses & commissions
- Fees for jury duty
- Unemployment compensation
- Discounts on purchases of employer's merchandise
- Fringe benefits such as use of company vehicle for personal purposes

Excluded:

- Health insurance paid by employer
- Group term life insurance up to $50,000 in coverage
- Employer-provided educational assistance
- Fringe benefits incurred for employer's benefit, such as housing provided to on-site hotel manager

Prizes & Awards

Generally taxable

Excluded from income:

1) Prize or award from employer

   Must be tangible personal property received for years of employment or safety

2) Scholarship or fellowship

   Must not be compensation for required services & must be spent for tuition by degree candidate

Interest

Included in income:

- Interest received or credited to taxpayer
- Interest accrued on zero-coupon bond
- Amortization of bond discount
- Interest on U.S. Treasury obligations
- Interest on tax refunds & insurance policies
- Interest portion of annuities received
- Interest on Series HH U.S. savings bonds

Excluded from income:

- Interest on state or municipal bonds
- Interest earned on qualified higher education bonds
- Interest on series EE U.S. savings bonds is reported when bonds mature

Dividends

Generally included in gross income

- Ordinary income distributions from Real Estate Investment Trusts (REITs) are taxed as ordinary income

- Capital gain distributions from REITs are taxed as long-term capital gains

Excluded from income:

- Stock dividends

- Dividends received from an S corporation

- Dividends received on a life insurance policy

- Dividends received from mutual funds investing in tax-exempt bonds

Other Income

Additional items included in gross income:
- Rents & royalties including rent collected in advance & nonrefundable deposits
- Discount on stock option upon exercise
- Injury awards for punitive damages or lost profits
- 85% of social security benefits of high income taxpayers
- State tax refunds if originally claimed as an itemized deduction
- Proceeds from a traditional IRA if contributions were deducted
- Alimony received in cash provided it terminates upon recipient's death

Additional items excluded from gross income:
- Damages received for physical injury or lost wages
- Workers' compensation benefits
- Social security received by low income taxpayers
- Portion of traditional IRA or pension withdrawal of prior nondeductible contributions
- All Roth IRA withdrawals
- Federal tax refunds
- Gifts & inheritances
- Life insurance proceeds

Adjustments for AGI

Items that may be deducted as adjustments for AGI include:

- **I**nterest on student loans
- **E**mployment tax – 50% of self-employment tax paid
- **M**oving expense
- **B**usiness expenses
- **R**ental & royalty expenses
- **A**limony paid
- **C**ontributions to retirement plans
- **E**arly withdrawal penalties on time deposits

As an alternative these items may appear as deductions of income from Schedule C or E

I EMBRACE adjustments that reduce AGI & lower taxes

Moving Expenses

Moving expenses are deducted if 3 conditions are met:

- Taxpayer moved due to change in location of job or business
- Taxpayer remains at new job for at least 9 months after the move
- Commute from old residence to new job at least 50 miles longer than commute from old residence to old job

Amounts deductible include direct costs of moving family & belongings:

- Airfares
- Shipping & temporary storage
- Transportation to new location (auto depreciation, gas, repairs, hotel)

Business Expenses

Include all reasonable business expenses

- Employee wages & payroll taxes
- Contributions to employee retirement plans
- Employee fringe benefits
- Interest on business loans
- Business taxes
- Casualty losses on business property
- 50% of meals & entertainment
- Bad debts when accounts are written off
- Gifts to customers & clients up to $25 per recipient per year

A net business loss reduces wages & business income, including net rental income, with any excess carried back or forward

Rent & Royalty Expenses

Expenses incurred on property generating rent or royalty income reduce the amount of rent or royalty income reported on Schedule E

- Depreciation or amortization
- Repairs
- Mortgage interest
- Property taxes
- Insurance

Rental & royalty properties are generally considered **passive activities**

- Any activity in which the investor does not materially participate
- Any real estate rental activity

Passive activity losses are not generally deductible

- Investor actively managing real estate rental property with AGI below $100,000 may deduct up to $25,000 per year (reduced by 50% of AGI - $100,000)
- Real estate broker or developer may deduct unlimited passive losses
- Nondeductible passive activity losses may be carried forward indefinitely or deducted when property sold

Contributions to Retirement Plans

Amounts deducted for contributions to retirement plans are subject to limitations:

- A self-employed taxpayer may deduct contributions up to 25% of net earnings up to $30,000 per year to a Keogh Plan

- An employee may exclude contributions (up to certain amount) contributed to a 401(k) plan

- A taxpayer may deduct up to $2,000 per year contributed to a traditional IRA, not to exceed earned income

- A married couple may deduct up to $2,000 each in contributions to traditional IRA accounts, even if only one spouse has earned income

In order to deduct traditional IRA contributions:

- The taxpayer may not participate in a pension plan at work

- The taxpayer's income is below a specified level

Roth IRAs

Individuals may contribute to a **Roth IRA** instead of a traditional IRA

- Not available to taxpayers with very high AGI

- Subject to same limitations

- Contributions are not deductible

- Neither contributions nor earnings subject to income tax when withdrawn

Withdrawn earnings are not taxable provided:

- Taxpayer is a least 59 ½ years old

- Taxpayer is disabled, deceased, or using withdrawal for first home purchase

Education IRAs

Taxpayer may establish **Education IRA**

- Not available to taxpayers with very high AGI

- May contribute up to $500 annually

- Must be on behalf of beneficiary under age 18

- Contributions not deductible

- Distributions not taxable if used for qualified higher education expenses

Additional For AGI Deductions

Penalties paid for early withdrawal, such as cashing a certificate of deposit before maturity, reduce AGI

Employees may be entitled to a **jury duty deduction**

- Applies when employer pays regular salary to employee during jury duty

- Employee recognizes both salary and jury duty fees as income

- Portion of jury duty fees remitted to employer are deducted in calculating AGI

Deductions

Standard Deduction

Basic amount depends on filing status

Additional deduction allowed for:

- Taxpayer is 65 or older
- Spouse is 65 or older
- Taxpayer is blind
- Spouse is blind

Deduction will be larger of standard deduction or total of itemized deductions

Taxpayers with high incomes may have the amount allowed for deductions reduced as a result of the **itemized deduction phase-out**

Itemized Deductions

Itemized deductions include amounts paid for:

- **C**ontributions
- **O**ther deductions
- **M**edical expenses
- **M**iscellaneous expenses
- **I**nterest
- **T**axes
- **T**heft or casualty losses

*Most taxpayers are **committ**ed to deducting the maximum amount allowed*

Contributions

Charitable contributions are deductible in the period:

- Payment is made to a recognized charity
- Property is given to a recognized charity
- Payment to a recognized charity is charged to a credit card

The amount of the deduction includes:

- Cash contributions
- Property at FMV
- Costs incurred in assisting the charity

The deduction does not include:

- The value of services performed
- The value of goods or services received in return for a contribution

The deduction is limited:

- Maximum deduction = 50% of AGI (30% if appreciated capital gain property)
- Nondeductible amounts may be carried forward up to 5 years

Other Itemized Deductions

Additional items may be claimed as itemized deductions, including:

- Gambling losses to the extent of winnings included in AGI

- Amortization of bond premium

Medical Expenses

Deductible medical expenses include:

- Fees to doctors, hospitals, & other providers of medical care
- Amounts paid for prescription drugs
- Premiums on health insurance coverage
- Transportation to doctor, hospital, or other provider

The deduction is reduced by:

- Reimbursements received or to be received from insurance
- 7 ½% of AGI

Miscellaneous Expenses

Deductible miscellaneous expenses include:

- Employee business expenses
- Investment costs
- Tax preparation fees

Employee business expenses include reasonable unreimbursed costs such as:

- Union or professional dues
- Trade journals
- Transportation to clients or customers
- Costs incurred on business trips including airfare, hotel, taxi, telephone, & 50% of meals & entertainment
- Uniforms
- Depreciation on business assets owned by employee
- Continuing education required to maintain employment

Employee business expenses do not include commuting to work or education obtained to qualify for a job (such as a CPA review course)

Miscellaneous Expenses (continued)

Deductible **investment expenses** include:

- Safe deposit box rent

- Subscriptions to investment periodicals

- Fees paid to financial advisors

- Cost of collecting income

Total miscellaneous expenses are reduced by 2% of AGI

Interest

Deductible interest includes interest on home mortgage loans

- Loans to buy, build, or improve the home up to $1,000,000
- Loans on equity up to $100,000
- Loans on 2nd homes are included provided the total falls within the limitations

Interest on personal indebtedness is not deductible:

- Car loans
- Credit card debt

Taxes

Deductible taxes include:

- State and local income taxes
- Property taxes
- Foreign taxes paid, unless foreign tax credit is elected

Certain taxes are not deductible

- Sales tax
- Inheritance tax
- Federal taxes, including federal income tax & FICA
- Fines
- Licensing & vehicle registration fees

Theft or Casualty Losses

Amount deductible based on decline in value of property based on theft or casualty

- May not exceed adjusted basis in property
- Must result from single loss rather than gradual decline in value

Each loss is reduced by:

- Insurance reimbursements received or expected
- $100

Total losses for the year are further reduced by

- 10% of AGI

Exemptions

Taxpayers may deduct personal exemptions and dependent exemptions

Taxpayers with high incomes may have the amount reduced as a result of the **exemption phase-out**

Personal Exemptions

A taxpayer may claim a personal exemption as a reduction of taxable income

- A married couple may take one exemption for each or 2 personal exemptions

- An individual who is a dependent on someone else's tax return may not claim a personal exemption

Dependent Exemptions

An exemption may be claimed for each dependent meeting 5 tests:

The dependent must have **gross income** lower than the exemption amount unless:

- The taxpayer's child under age 19

- A full-time student under age 24

The dependent must be a **relative** of the taxpayer or resides in the taxpayer's home throughout the year

The taxpayer provided over 50% of the dependent's **support**

The dependent must be a **citizen** or national of the US or a **resident** of the US, Canada, or Mexico

The dependent cannot be filing a **joint return**

Dependent Exemptions (continued)

When several people combine to provide over 50% of the dependent's support, only one may take the exemption dependent

- The parties must sign a **multiple support agreement**

- The party taking the exemption must provide at least 10% of the support

- The taxpayer must otherwise qualify to take the dependent exemption

Credits

Several credits may reduce a taxpayer's total tax

- Dependent care credit
- Credit for the aged & disabled
- Earned income credit
- Child tax credit
- Hope Scholarship credit
- Lifetime learning credit
- Foreign tax credit

Earned Income Credit

To qualify, taxpayer must meet 2 conditions:

- Taxpayer has earned income
- Taxpayer provides support for a dependent child or grandchild

The earned income credit is refundable

- Treated as if paid
- Results in refund if credit exceeds tax liability

Credit for Aged or Disabled

Allowed for individuals with low income who are over 65 or permanently disabled

Dependent Care Credit

A credit is allowed for:

- 20% X amounts paid to care for a qualifying dependent
- Maximum credit = $2,400 for 1 dependent, $4,800 for 2 or more dependents
- Taxpayers with AGI ≤ $10,000 may take credit of 30% (reduced by 1% for each $2,000 above AGI of $10,000 until reduced to 20%)

Dependent must be either:

- Child under age 13
- Disabled spouse or dependent of any age

Self-Employment Tax

Employer & employees pay payroll taxes

- Medicare tax paid equally on 100% of wages
- FICA paid equally on wages up to a base amount

Self-employed individuals pay employer's & employee's shares

- Income from self-employment X rate = self-employment tax
- 50% of self-employment tax is adjustment in determining AGI

Alternative Minimum Tax (AMT)

	Taxable income
±	Adjustments & preferences
=	Alternative minimum taxable income (AMTI)
−	Exemption
=	Base
X	Tax rate
=	Tentative minimum tax
−	Regular tax liability
=	AMT

AMT (continued)

The primary adjustments to income in calculating AMTI are:

- **S**tandard deduction
- **I**nterest on home equity loans
- **M**edical expenses under 10% of AGI
- **P**ersonal and dependent exemptions
- **L**ocal and state tax deductions
- **E**mployee and investment expenses subject to the 2% of AGI rule

The primary preferences are:

- **P**rivate activity bond interest
- **I**ncentive stock options
- **E**xcess depreciation

*It's as **simple** as **pie** to remember the adjustments and preferences for AMTI*

AMT (continued)

AMTI is reduced by the **exemption** amount

Exemption = Basic amount − 25% X (AMTI − $150,000)

Married joint exemption is $45,000 - 25% X (AMTI - $150,000)

Single exemption is $33,750 - 25% X (AMTI - $112,500)

Resulting base amount X tax rate = tentative minimum tax

- 26% X 1st $175,000

- 28% X (Base amount - $175,000)

Tentative minimum tax − regular income tax = AMT adjustment

- If tentative minimum tax > regular income tax − difference increases tax amount

- If tentative minimum tax < regular income tax − difference is an AMT credit

AMT credits reduce regular tax to extent of AMT paid in previous years

Tax Payments

Tax payments include

- Excess payroll taxes withheld
- Federal income taxes withheld
- Estimated tax payments

Excess Payroll Taxes

Employees with 2 or more employers

- Total wages may exceed base amount for FICA
- Maximum FICA = base amount X FICA rate
- Excess withheld treated as estimated tax payment

Penalties for Late Payment

Penalty imposed for late payment of taxes unless:

- Underpayment for year < $1000
- Payments ≥ 90% of current year's liability
- Taxes paid ≥ 100% of prior year's liability (> 100% for taxpayers with AGI > $150,000)

Filing Status

A taxpayer's filing status will determine the rates and various amounts used in computing taxable income & the tax liability

Married Couples

Choice of 2 alternatives

- Married, filing jointly
- Married, filing separately

Must be married as of last day of year or date of death if one spouse died during the year

Unmarried Individuals

Choice of 3 alternatives

1) Qualified widow or widower

    - Must be providing support for a dependent child

    - Available for 2 years after death of spouse

    - Joint return was filed while spouse was alive

2) Head of household

    - Generally must be providing support for dependent living in the same home for more than ½ of year

    - Taxpayer's unmarried child or grandchild living with taxpayer need not be dependent

    - Taxpayer's parent need not live in same home if supported by taxpayer

3) Single – all others

Carryover Rules

	Carryback	*Carryforward*
Charitable contributions	No	5 years
Net operating losses	2 years	20 years
Net capital losses		
Corporations	3 years	5 years
Individuals	No	Indefinitely
Investment interest	No	Indefinitely
Net passive losses	No	Indefinitely, or claimed when investment sold
Net gambling losses	No	No

Tax Return Schedules

An individual files their tax return on a **form 1040** along with some or all of the following supplementary schedules:

- **Sched A** – Itemized Deductions
- **Sched B** – Interest & Dividend Income
- **Sched C** – Profit or Loss From Business
- **Sched D** – Capital Gains & Losses
- **Sched E** – Supplemental Income & Loss
- **Form 4797** – Sale of Business Property
- **Sched 1116** – Foreign Tax Credit

Taxation of Exempt Organizations

Types of Exempt Organizations

Organizations that can apply & be approved for exempt status include:
- Nonprofit religious, educational, scientific, or charitable organizations
- Political organizations
- Labor unions
- Pension plans
- Civic organizations
- Condominium associations
- Social clubs

May not attempt to influence legislation or support a political candidate

An exempt organization can be a corporation or a trust:
- Private foundation – if less than 1/3 of support is from general public
- Public charity – if 1/3 or more of support is from general public

Reporting by Exempt Organizations

Annual reports to IRS

- Names of significant contributors

- Amounts contributed by each

- Gross receipts & disbursements for year

Organizations exempt from reporting

- Churches

- Organizations with gross receipts < $25,000

Unrelated Business Income (UBI)

Taxation of UBI

UBI is income unrelated to organization's main purpose

UBI
- Expenses
- $1,000 exemption
= Taxable UBI

Non-UBI Activities

Certain activities are never considered UBI activities

- Occasional activities
- Dividends, interest, & royalties
- Profits on sales to members
- Profits on sales of contributed merchandise
- Profits on activities of volunteers
- Profits from legal games of chance

Filing & Tax Preparers

Filing Requirements

Who Must File

Individuals with:

- Gross income > personal exemption + standard deduction

- Self-employment income $\geq$ $400

- Gross income > standard deduction (if dependent)

When to File

Normal returns due on or before April 15

- May be extended to August 15 (automatic)
- May be further extended to October 15 (with IRS approval)

Amended returns due by later of:

- 3 years after original date (including extensions granted)
- 2 years after taxes actually paid

Claims for Refunds

Overstatement of income on original return

- Amended return on form 1040X
- Due 3 years after original due date (including extensions granted)
- Due 2 years after payment of taxes, if later

Statutes of Limitations

Time IRS has to impose additional taxes & penalties on taxpayer

- Begins day after return is filed or due date including extensions, whichever is later
- Time period depends on nature of error

Taxpayer Error	Time Period
Simple negligence	3 years
Gross negligence (omission ≥ 25% of income)	6 years
Fraud or failure to file	No limit

Tax Return Due Dates

Assuming taxable year ended December 31:

Tax Return	Due Date
Individual income tax return Amended individual income tax return Gift tax return Trust income tax return Estate income tax return Partnership tax return	April 15 of following year
Corporate tax return S corporation tax return	March 15 of following year
S corporation status election	March 15 of current year
Exempt organization tax return	May 15 of following year
Estate tax return	9 months after date of death

Tax Preparer Penalties

Minor violations - $50 fine:
- Disclose confidential information on client's return
- Endorse or deposit client's refund for preparer's benefit
- Fail to sign return as preparer
- Fail to provide client with copy of filed return
- Fail to keep copies of client returns for at least 3 years
- Fail to keep list for at least 3 years of employees preparing returns

Major violations:
- Knowingly make claim with no realistic possibility of success without disclosing claim as frivolous to IRS - $250 penalty
- Intentionally or recklessly disregard tax rules to reduce client liability - $1,000 penalty

No violation:
- Claim good faith position with realistic possibility of success
- Use estimates when client did not maintain adequate records
- Rely on information supplied by client not appearing incorrect or inconsistent

Taxation of Estates & Trusts

Estates

Results from death of individual

- Assets become part of estate
- Investments generate income
- Estate taxed on earnings

Trusts

Types of Trusts

Simple trusts

- Must distribute all income each year
- May not make charitable contributions

Complex trusts – all others

Trust Operations

Grantor (creator)
Places assets into trust

↓

```
┌─────────────────────────────┐
│          Trustee            │
│    Oversees trust's assets  │
└─────────────────────────────┘
```

Income beneficiary
Receives net earnings of trust

Remainderman
Receives remaining principal
(corpus) upon termination

Taxation of Trusts

Grantor (revocable) trust

- Creator has right to withdraw assets at any time

- Earnings taxed to creator (as if trust did not exist)

Irrevocable trust

- Creator generally may not withdraw assets

- Trust taxed separately from creator or beneficiaries

Computing Taxable Income of Trusts & Estates

    Gross income

\-   Deductions

\-   Exemption

\=   Taxable income

Gross Income

Same rules as for individuals

Includes:

- Rents
- Dividends
- Interest
- Capital gains

Deductions

Generally similar to those available to individual

In addition:

- Charitable contributions – No limit on amount
- Management fees – Fee paid to trustee or executor

  Trust or estate may have nontaxable income

  Proportionate amount of fee not deductible

- Distributions paid – Amounts paid to beneficiaries

Exemption

Estate - $600

Simple trust - $300

Complex trust - $100

Distributable Net Income (DNI)

DNI is maximum amount trustee may pay to income beneficiary

- Remainder maintained in principal for remainderman
- Includes most income & expense items on trust tax return
- Includes municipal bond interest
- Does not include net capital gains (principal)

Taxation of Beneficiaries

Not taxed on inheritance of estate property

Taxed on distributions of income up to DNI

Filing Issues

	Trusts	*Estates*
Reporting period	Calendar year	Fiscal year Begins on date of death
Tax return due date	April 15 of following year	3 ½ months after close of year
Estimated quarterly tax payments	Required	Not required for 1st 2 years Required after
Exemption amount	Simple - $300 Complex - $100	$600

Estate & Gift Tax

Total taxable gifts during lifetime

+ Total taxable estate

= Total taxable transfers

X Tax rates

= Tentative tax amount

- The unified credit

- Other credits

= Tax due

Taxable Gifts

Include:

- Gifts of cash or property
- Discount on sale of property to family member
- Reduction in interest on loans to family members at low rates

Exclude:

- Donations to political organizations & charities
- Discounts given in negotiated transaction between independent parties
- Parent's support of minor child
- Amounts paid to college, doctor, or hospital for other party's tuition or medical care

Reduce by:

- Marital deduction
- Gift exclusions

Taxable Gifts (continued)

Marital Deduction - Property given to a spouse is not taxable if spouse obtains either:

- Complete ownership of property
- Right as trust beneficiary to income from property for remainder of beneficiary's life (Qualified Terminable Interest Property trust or QTIP trust)

Gift Exclusions

May exclude up to $10,000 per recipient per year

Married couple making gift-splitting election may exclude up to $20,000 per recipient per year

Recipient must generally receive present interest in gift

- Recipient obtains ownership
- Recipient obtains guaranteed right to income from property

If recipient obtains future interest, present value of gift is fully taxable

Taxable Estate

Gross estate – All property owned at time of death

Includes:

- Proceeds from life insurance policies where deceased could change beneficiary

- Assets held in revocable trust

- Half of property owned jointly with spouse

- Proportionate share of cost of property held jointly with other parties

Valued at lower of:

- Fair value at date of death

- Fair value 6 months after date of death (alternate valuation date)

  If alternate valuation date is selected, assets distributed during 6 months valued at date of distribution

Taxable Estate (continued)

Reduce by:

- Charitable bequests
- Marital deduction
- Family-owned business
- Expenses & liabilities

Charitable bequests – Unlimited deduction for amounts left to charitable organizations

Marital deduction – Unlimited amount subject to same rules as gifts

Family-owned business – Up to $1,300,000 in value of a family-owned business if transferred to a member of the decedent's family or an employee of at least 10 years prior to the decedent's death

Taxable Estate (continued)

Expenses & Liabilities – Deductions for

- Liabilities incurred prior to death

- Funeral costs

- Administrative fees

- Medical expenses

Administrative fees may be deducted as either a liability on the estate tax return or an expense deduction on the estate's income tax return

Medical expenses incurred during decedent's lifetime may be deducted as claims against the estate or as a medical deduction on the decedent's income tax return if paid within one year of death

Tax Due

Tentative Amount

	Total taxable transfers
X	Tax rates (from table)
=	Tentative tax amount

Unified Credit

Tentative amount reduced by unified gift & estate tax credit

- Credit designed to make estates up to certain limits nontaxable
- Limit is $675,000 in 2000 & 2001, $700,000 in 2002 & 2003, $850,000 in 2004, $950,000 in 2005, & $1,000,000 in 2006 & after

Other Credits

Credit for estate or inheritance tax paid to state

Credit for death tax paid to foreign country on real estate owned in that country

Taxes paid on prior transfers

Property Received by Inheritance or Gift

Inheritance

Not income to recipient

Basis – Fair market value reported on estate return

- Value at date of death
- Value at alternate valuation date
- Value at date of distribution if between the 2

Holding period – automatically long-term

Gift

Not income to recipient

Appreciated property - basis & holding period same as donor

Depreciated property

- If sold at loss – basis = value on date of gift

- If sold at gain – basis = same as donor

- If sales price between value on date of gift & donor's basis – no gain or loss

Property Dispositions

Realized Gain or Loss

    Amount realized
  − Adjusted basis
  = Realized gain or loss

Amount Realized

    Cash received
  + FMV of property received
  + Net debt relief
  - Direct selling expenses
  = Amount realized

Net debt relief = liabilities transferred − liabilities assumed

Adjusted Basis

	Initial basis
+	Improvements
-	Depreciation
-	Costs recovered
±	Adjustments
=	Adjusted basis

Initial Basis

Property converted from personal use to business or investment use	Lower of actual basis or FMV on date of conversion
Inherited property	FMV at date of death or alternate valuation date (6 months later)
Appreciated gift property	Carryover basis (donor's basis)

Depreciation Recapture

Does not apply to leases or sales of real estate

            Realized gain

    -    Depreciation recapture (ordinary income)

    =   Capital gain

Amount of depreciation recapture:

- Realized gain < accumulated depreciation – use amount of gain
- Realized gain ≥ accumulated depreciation – use accumulated depreciation

Taxation of Gains & Losses

Tax Treatment

Ordinary assets • Inventory • Business receivables • Self-created artistic works	Regular rates
Section 1231 assets • Depreciable or amortizable business assets • Land used in business	Net gains - LTCG Net losses - ordinary

Capital assets all others	INDIVIDUALS: LTCG – Special rates
	               STCG – Regular rates
	Net loss – Max of $3,000 during current year. Carryforward indefinite.
	CORPORATIONS:
	  Net loss - not deductible
	  Carryback 2 years. Carryforward 20 years.

Related Party Sales

Related parties include:

- Child, grandchild, parent, grandparent, spouse, brother, sister

- Corporation or partnership where ownership > 50%

Tax effects:

- Losses – not deductible by seller

- Buyer's basis – purchase price

- Subsequent gains – taxed to extent subsequent gain > nondeductible loss

Special Transactions

Type of Transaction	Special Rule
Sale of personal assets	Losses not recognized
Wash sales – Taxpayer acquires stock within 30 days of selling same stock	Losses not recognized
Related party transactions	Losses not recognized
Like-kind exchanges	Losses not recognized Gains recognized to extent of boot

Involuntary conversions
  Similar replacement property acquired within 2 years of year-end for casualty or theft or 3 years for condemnation
  Election to not report gain filed
	If cost of replacement property
	  ≥ proceeds – no gain recognized
	If cost of replacement property
	  < proceeds – gain recognized =
	     Proceeds
	    - Cost or replacement property

Special Transactions (continued)

Type of Transaction	*Special Rule*
Installment sale	Gain recognized Cash collected ÷ Total sales price X Total gain
Sale of principal residence If taxpayer lived in home at least two of prior five years	Same rules as involuntary conversion Up to $250,000 of gain excluded

S Corporations

Formation of S Corporations

Requirements

S corporation status requires all of the following:

- # of shareholders $\leq$ 75

- Shareholders are only individuals, estates, & some trusts

- Only 1 class of stock

Election

Corporation must elect S corporation status

- All stockholders must elect unanimously

- Election due during 1st 2 ½ months of tax year

Conversion To S Corporation

An S corporation is not generally taxed on its income

When a taxable corporation elects S corporation status, it may be subject to:

1) Built-in gain tax – Applies when company sells appreciated assets within 10 years of election

   S corporation pays tax at corporate rates on built-in gain

   > Appreciated value at election
   > - Basis in asset
   > = Built-in gain

2) Tax on excess passive investment income – Applies when investment income > 25% of revenues from all sources

   S corporation pays tax at corporate rates on investment income in excess of 25%

Taxation of S Corporations

S corporation's not taxable entities

Must prepare:

- Information tax return
- Form K-1 indicating shareholder's share of income & expenses

S Corporation's income & expenses **pass through** to individual shareholders

- Each item is combined with comparable items recognized by the shareholder
- Combined amounts are subject to the same limitations as the individual amounts would have been

S Corporation Earnings

Pass Through Item	Tax Treatment
Capital gains & losses	Gains taxed at capital gain rates Losses subject to $3,000 maximum deduction
Section 1231 gains & losses	Gains treated as capital gains Losses treated as ordinary
Charitable contributions	Subject to limitation $\leq 50\%$ AGI
Interest & dividend income & related expenses	Investment expenses deductible to extent of investment income
Net rent & royalty income	Subject to passive activity loss limitations

S Corporation Earnings (continued)

Pass Through Item	Tax Treatment
Section 179 deduction	Subject to limitation that increases to $25,000 in year 2003
Tax credits	Limited to tax liability
Tax-exempt income & related expenses	Income not taxable to shareholders Expenses not deductible by shareholder
Tax preferences & adjustments	Used to compute shareholder's AMT
All remaining items	Ordinary income or loss Losses limited to shareholder's investment

Shareholder's Basis

A shareholder's basis in S corporation stock can be computed as follows:

  Initial basis
± Share of income or loss
- Distributions received
= Basis in stock

Initial basis = cash and basis of property contributed by shareholder to acquire stock

Share of income or loss = shareholder's proportionate share of all of corporation's income & expenses, regardless of nature

Distributions received are a return of capital and are not taxed to the shareholder

Termination of S Corporation Status

Either of the following will cause a corporation to lose its S corporation status

- Shareholders ≥ 50% vote to revoke election

- No longer eligible based on requirements

Once terminated, corporation must wait 5 years to elect again

Partnership Taxation

Formation of Partnerships

Contribution of Assets

When a partner contributes cash or property for a partnership interest, it is nontaxable

- Partner's basis in partnership = basis in assets contributed
- Partnership's basis in assets = partner's basis (carryover basis)

Contribution of Services

When a partner contributes services for a partnership interest, it is taxable

- Partner has income & basis in partnership = FMV
- Partnership recognizes expense & contribution = FMV

Tax Year

Based on tax years of individual or corporate partners

1) Same as tax year of partner owning > 50%

2) No partner owns > 50%, same as tax year of partners owning ≥ 5% if all have same tax year

3) If all partners with ≥ 5% do not have same tax year, use year that results in least deferral of income

Taxation of Partnerships

Partnership's are not taxable entities

Similar to S Corporations

- Complete information return
- Prepare form K-1 for each partner indicating share of income & expenses
- Partnership's income & expenses pass through to partner
- Partner combines with similar items earned or incurred individually
- Combined amounts subject to normal limitations

Guaranteed Payments to Partners

Guaranteed payments to partners are amounts partners are entitled to regardless of partnership's profit or loss

May be:

- Salary for services performed

- Interest based on capital investment in partnership

Taxed as follows:

- Partner recognizes as ordinary income

- Partnership deducts in calculating partnership ordinary income or loss

Partner's Basis

        Initial basis

 ±   Partner's share of income or loss

 -    Distributions

 +   Partner's share of partnership liabilities

 -    Liabilities contributed to partnership

 =   Partner's basis in partnership

Initial basis = cash, property, & services contributed

Partner's share of income or loss = partner's proportionate share of all of partnership's income & expenses, regardless of nature

Distributions = cash & property distributed to partner

Partner's proportionate share of partnership's liabilities are added to basis

Partner's liabilities that are transferred to the partnership reduce basis

Distributions

Nonliquidating Distributions

Cash distributed

- Reduces partner's basis

- Taxable to extent distribution > basis

Property distributed

- Basis to partner = lower of partnership's basis in property or partner's basis in partnership

- Basis in partnership reduced by partner's basis in property

- No income recognized

Liquidating Distributions

Distributions to partner upon withdrawal from partnership

Cash distributions

- Difference between amount received & partner's basis in partnership = gain or loss
- Basis in partnership = $0

Property distributions

- Basis to partner = basis in partnership
- Basis in partnership = $0
- No gain or loss recognized

Sale of Partnership Interest

Determining Gain or Loss

       Sales proceeds
-    Basis in partnership
=   Gain or loss

Proceeds = cash received + FMV of property received + debts assumed by buyer

Taxation of Gains & Losses

Gain or loss divided into 2 segments:

- Partner's share of appreciation in partnership's receivables & inventory is ordinary

- Resulting amount is capital gain or loss

Termination

Partnerships terminate when either:

- Partnership stops doing business
- Ownership interests > 50% are sold within a 12 month period

Cost & Managerial Accounting

Cost Estimation, Cost Determination, & Cost Drivers

Calculating Total Costs

Total costs = fixed costs + variable costs

$$y = A + Bx$$

y = total cost (dependent variable)

A = total fixed costs

B = variable cost per unit

x = # of units (independent variable)

Various methods are used to determine the variable cost per unit & total fixed costs

Cost Drivers

Units represent volume of cost driver

- Cost driver can be any variable that has greatest influence on cost

- Examples include volume of production, hours worked, miles driven, or machine hours

High-Low Method

4 steps in estimating variable cost per unit & total fixed costs

1) Highest volume   Total cost   # of units
   Lowest volume   Total cost   # of units
       Difference   Cost   # of units

2) Variable cost per unit = difference in cost ÷ difference in # of units

3) Total variable costs (at either level) = variable cost per unit X # of units

4) Fixed costs (at either level) = total costs - total variable costs

Regression Analysis

Coefficient of correlation (R) indicates relationship between dependent & independent variable:

- R = 1   – Strong direct relationship

- 1 > R > 0   – Direct relationship, not as strong

- R = 0   – No relationship

- 0 > R > -1 – Indirect relationship, not as strong

- R = -1   – Strong indirect relationship

Company will use cost drive with strongest direct or indirect relationship

Cost Classifications

Product & period costs

	Product	Period
Direct materials (DM)	X	
Direct labor (DL)	X	
Manufacturing overhead (MOH)	X	
Selling, general, & administrative expenses (S, G, & A)		X

Prime & conversion costs

	Prime	Conversion
DM	X	
DL	X	X
MOH		X

Variable & fixed costs

	Variable	Fixed
DM	X	
DL	X	
MOH	X	X
S, G, & A	X	X

Spoilage & Scrap

Different types of unused units or materials have different accounting treatments:

Normal spoilage – product cost (added to cost of good units)

Abnormal spoilage – period cost (charged against income in period

Scrap – generally charged to cost of goods manufactured

Proceeds from sale of scrap:

- Additional income
- Reduce cost of sales
- Reduce manufacturing overhead
- Reduce cost of specific job

Job Costing, Process Costing, & Activity Based Costing

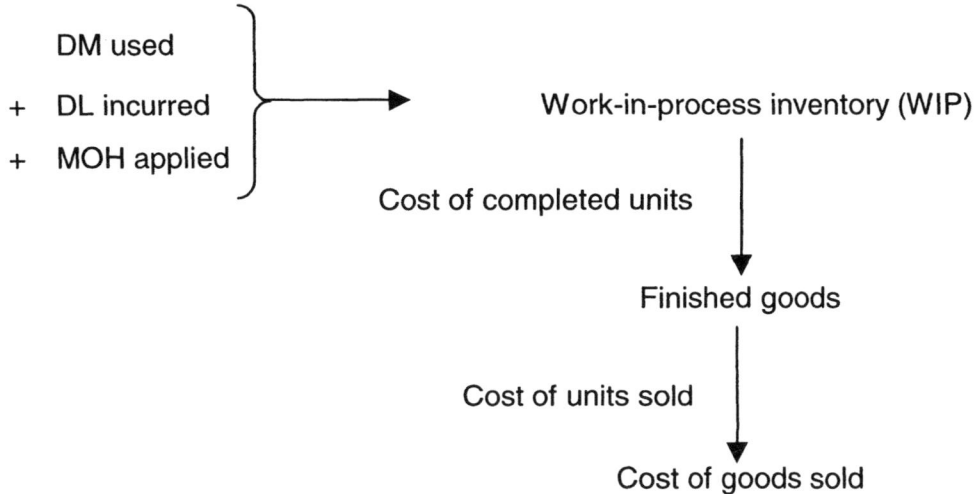

DM used
+ DL incurred
+ MOH applied

→ Work-in-process inventory (WIP)

Cost of completed units

↓

Finished goods

Cost of units sold

↓

Cost of goods sold

Manufacturing Overhead

1) Calculate the predetermined overhead rate (POHR)
   Estimated variable MOH for period
   + Estimated fixed MOH for period
   = Estimated total MOH for period
   ÷ Estimated # of units for period (cost driver)
   = Predetermined overhead rate (POHR) – often split into fixed & variable rates
2) Apply MOH to WIP
   Actual # of units for period (cost driver)
   X POHR
   = MOH Applied
3) Determine under-applied or over-applied MOH
   - Actual MOH > MOH applied – MOH under-applied
   - Actual MOH < MOH applied – MOH over-applied
4) Dispose of under-applied or over-applied MOH
   - Generally added to or deducted from COGS
   - May be charged or credited directly to income
   - May be allocated to WIP, finished goods, & COGS

Activity Based Costing (ABC)

Method of analyzing & reducing MOH

- MOH segregated into pools

- Cost driver identified for each pool

- MOH applied using multiple rates

Identifies costs that are nonvalue adding

- Can be used to reduce overhead

- Identify & minimize nonvalue adding costs

Also used to allocate service department costs

Activity Based Costing (ABC) (continued)

Under step allocation method
- Services departments allocated beginning with those serving most other departments
- Allocation based on that department's cost driver
- Costs allocated to all remaining service departments & production departments
- Costs not charged back to service departments already allocated
- Process complete when only production departments remain

	Service departments				*Production departments*	
	#1	*#2*	*#3*	*#4*	*#1*	*#2*
Costs	$	$	$	$	$	$
Allocation	($)	$	$	$	$	$
Subtotal	0	$	$	$	$	$
Allocation		($)	$	$	$	$
Subtotal		0	$	$	$	$
Allocation			($)	$	$	$
Subtotal			0	$	$	$
Allocation				($)	$	$
Total				0	$	$

Job Order Costing

Used when units are relatively expensive & costs can be identified to units or batches

- DM, DL, & MOH applied charged to WIP

- Cost of completed units removed from WIP & charged to finished goods

- Cost of units sold removed from finished goods & charged to COGS

Process Costing

Used when units are relatively inexpensive & costs cannot be identified to units or batches

- DM, DL, & MOH applied charged to WIP

- Calculates average cost of equivalent units produced during period

- Average costs used to transfer from WIP to finished goods & from finished goods to COGS

Calculating equivalent units

- Costs incurred at beginning of process – equivalent units = units X 100%

- Costs incurred at end of process – equivalent units = units X 0%

- Costs incurred uniformly – equivalent units = units X % complete

- Costs incurred at particular point

  If units reached that point – equivalent units = units X 100%

  If units haven't reached that point – equivalent units = units X 0%

Process Costing (continued)

Process costing – **weighted average**

1)   Costs in beginning WIP
  + Costs incurred during period
  = Total costs to be allocated

2)   Units completed during period
  + Equivalent units in ending WIP
  = Total equivalent production

3)   Total costs to be allocated
  ÷ Total equivalent production
  = Average cost per equivalent unit

2)   Units completed during period
  X Average cost per equivalent unit
  = Amount allocated to finished goods

3)   Equivalent units in ending inventory
  X Average cost per equivalent unit
  = Amount allocated to ending WIP

Process Costing (continued)

Process costing – **FIFO**

1)   Determine costs incurred during period

2)   Units in beginning WIP
   -    Equivalent units in beginning WIP
   =   Equivalent units required to complete beginning WIP

3)   Equivalent units required to complete beginning WIP
   ÷   Units started & completed during period X 100%
   +   Equivalent units in ending WIP
   =   Total equivalent production

4)   Costs incurred during period
   ÷   Total equivalent production
   =   Average cost per equivalent unit

5)   Costs in beginning WIP
   +   Units started & completed X Average cost per equivalent unit
   =   Amount allocated to finished goods

6)   Equivalent units in ending WIP
   X   Average cost per equivalent unit
   =   Amount allocated to ending WIP

Budgeting & Standard Costing

Flexible Budgeting

Used to estimate revenue, costs, a group of costs, or profits at various levels of activity

- Applies when operating within a relevant range
- Total fixed costs remain the same at all levels within range
- Variable costs per unit of activity remains the same within range

Master & Static Budgets

Static budget – budget as specific level of activity

- Can be for division of company

- Can be for company as a whole

Master budget – static budget for company as a whole

Master budget generally includes:

- Operating budget

- Budgeted cash flows

- Budgeted financial statements

Preparing a master budget

1) Estimate sales volume

2) Use sales volume to estimate revenues

3) Use collection history to estimate collections

4) Estimate cost of sales based on units sold

5) Use current finished goods inventory, budgeted ending inventory, & cost of sales to estimate units to be manufactured

6) Use units manufactured to estimate material needs, labor costs, & overhead costs

7) Use material needs, current raw materials inventory, & budgeted ending inventory to budget purchases

8) Use purchase terms to estimate payments

9) Analyze expense & payment patterns to complete operating & cash flow budgets

Budgeting Material Purchases & Payments

    Units sold

\+ Budgeted increase in finished goods

\- Budgeted decrease in finished goods

\= Units to be manufactured

X Units of raw material per unit of finished goods

\= Units of raw material required for production

\+ Budgeted increase in raw materials

\- Budgeted decrease in raw materials

\= **Budgeted raw material purchases**

\+ Budgeted decrease in accounts payable

\- Budgeted increase in accounts payable

\= **Budgeted payments for raw materials**

Standard Costing

Material Variances

Standard cost (units produced X std qty per unit X std cost per unit)
- Actual material cost
= Total material variance

Material price variance (MPV)
+ Material usage variance (MUV)
= Total material variance

MPV = act qty X (std pr − act pr)   MUV = std pr X (std qty − act qty)

Standard Costing (continued)

Labor Variances

      Standard cost (units produced X std hrs per unit X std rate per hr)
-   Actual labor cost
=   Total labor variance

                  Labor rate variance (LRV)
            +   Labor efficiency variance (LEV)
            =   Total labor variance

LRV = act qty X (std rate − act rate)   LEV = std rate X (std hrs − act hrs)

Standard Costing (continued)

Overhead Variances

　　　Overhead applied (std hrs X total POHR)
-　　Actual overhead cost
=　　Total overhead variance

　　　　　　　Overhead volume variance (OVV)
　　　+　　Overhead efficiency variance (OEV)
　　　+　　Overhead spending variance (OSV)
　　　=　　Total overhead variance

Std hrs X POHR (fixed)	Std hrs X POHR (variable)	Act hrs X POHR (total)
-　Budgeted fixed OH	-　Act hrs X POHR (variable)	+　Budgeted fixed OH
= OVV	= OEV	-　Act OH
		= OSV

Inventory Planning & Control & Just-In-Time Purchasing

Economic Order Quantity (EOQ)

Minimizes total of order cost & carrying cost

- Order cost – cost of placing an order or starting a production run

- Carrying cost – cost of having inventory on hand

$$EOQ = \sqrt{2AP/S}$$

A = Annual demand in units

P = Cost of placing an order or beginning a production run

S = Cost of carrying 1 unit in inventory for 1 period

Reorder Point & Safety Stock

Reorder point

- Units in inventory when order should be placed

- Avg daily demand X avg lead time = reorder point

Safety stock

- Extra units in inventory when placing order in case demand or lead time > avg

- Avoids costs associated with running out of stock

- Max daily demand X max lead time − reorder point = safety stock

Just-In-Time (JIT) Purchasing

Costs reduced through:
- Reduction in inventory quantities
- Elimination of nonvalue adding operations
- Most appropriate when order cost low & carrying cost high

Requires high quality control standards
- Efficient system minimizing defective units
- Corrections made as defects occur
- Fewer vendors & suppliers

Problems of JIT system:
- Difficult to find suppliers able to accommodate
- High shipping costs due to smaller orders
- Potential problems due to delays in deliveries

May use backflush approach
- All manufacturing costs charged to COGS
- Costs allocated from COGS to inventories at reporting dates

Responsibility Accounting & Performance Evaluation

Company divisions may be:

- Cost centers – manager responsible for costs incurred
- Profit centers – manager responsible for costs & revenues
- Investment centers – manager responsible for costs, revenues, & capital investments

Performance Evaluation

Measures of performance of investment center

- Profit margin = operating profits ÷ sales

- Asset turnover = sales ÷ assets

- Return on investment = operating profits ÷ assets

- Return on investment = profit margin X asset turnover

- Residual income = operating profits − imputed interest on assets

Transfer Pricing

Transfer price – price at which products are transferred from one department to another within the same company

Possible transfer prices
- Actual cost
- Market value
- Cost + profit
- Negotiated amount
- Standard cost

Transfer from cost center to profit center – generally use standard variable cost

- Cost center evaluated based on comparing standard variable cost to actual cost

- Profit center not affected by performance of cost center

Nonfinancial Measures

Improve efficiency by minimizing:

- Throughput time

  Average time for unit to pass through system

  Throughput time = avg units in inventory ÷ units manufactured/day

- Time of setting up production runs

  Setup time for machine ÷ total production time

- Units requiring rework

  Units requiring rework ÷ total units completed

Quality Control

Designed to improve performance & prevent defective products

Prevention costs – prevent product failure

- Use high quality materials

- Inspect production process

- Train employees

- Maintain machines

Appraisal or detection costs – detect product failure

- Inspect samples of finished goods

- Obtain information from customers

Quality Control (continued)

Poor quality control results in increased costs

Internal failure costs

- Scrap resulting from wasted materials
- Reworking units to correct defects
- Reinspection & retesting after rework

External failure costs

- Warranty costs
- Dealing with customer complaints
- Product liability
- Marketing to improve image
- Lost sales

Variable & Absorption Costing

Absorption costing
- Used for financial statements

- Inventory includes DM + DL + variable MOH + fixed MOH

Variable costing
- Used for internal purposes only
- Inventory includes DM + DL + variable MOH

Absorption costing		**Variable costing**	
	Sales		Sales
-	Cost of sales	-	Variable costs
=	Gross profit	=	Contribution margin
-	S, G, & A expenses	-	Fixed costs
=	Operating income	=	Operating income

Difference = Change in inventory X fixed overhead per unit

Cost-Volume-Profit Analysis

	Sales price per unit		Contrib margin per unit
-	Variable cost per unit	÷	Sales price per unit
=	Contrib margin per unit	=	Contrib margin ratio

Units   **_Dollars_**

Breakeven

	Fixed costs		Fixed costs
÷	Contrib margin per unit	÷	Contrib margin ratio
=	Breakeven in units	=	Breakeven in dollars

Profit as fixed amount

	Fixed costs + desired profit		Fixed costs + desired profit
÷	Contrib margin per unit	÷	Contrib margin ratio
=	Units required to earn desired profit	=	Sales dollars required to earn desired profit

Profit as percentage of sales

	Fixed costs		Fixed costs
÷	Contrib margin - profit per unit	÷	(Contrib margin – profit) ÷ sales price
=	Units required to earn profit ratio =		Sales required to earn profit ratio

Margin of Safety

- Sales volume > breakeven point
- Margin of safety = amount by which sales can be reduced to achieve breakeven

When costs increase:

- Breakeven point is increased
- Margin of safety is decreased

Graphical Approach to Breakeven

AC = profit for product at various levels of production
B = breakeven point
OA = fixed costs
DE = loss at production point D (below breakeven)
FG = profit at production point G (above breakeven)
OA ÷ OB = contribution margin
FG ÷ BG = contribution margin

Joint Products & By-Products

Joint Product Costing

Joint products – 2 or more products resulting from same process

- Joint product costs – costs incurred before products separated
- Split-off point – earliest point at which products can be separated
- Sales value – amount each product can be sold for at earliest point of sale
- Separable costs – costs incurred after split-off point before products can be sold
- Relative sales value – sales value – separable costs

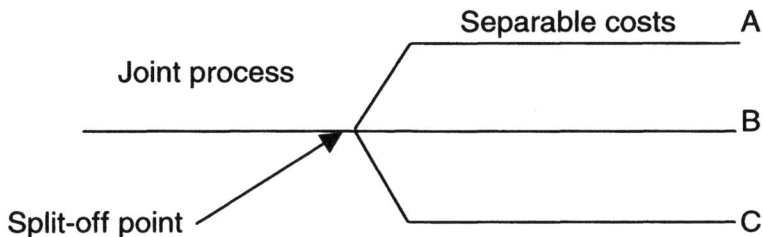

Joint Product Costing (continued)

Allocating joint product costs – relative sales value method

1) Calculate relative sales value for each joint product

2) Add together to calculate total relative sales value

3) Calculate ratio of relative sales value for each joint product to total relative sales value

4) Multiply ratio for each product by joint product costs

5) Result is amount of joint product costs to be allocated to each product

Accounting for By-Products

Revenues from sale of by-product generally reduce cost of other products

1) Determine revenues from sale of by-products

2) Reduce by separable costs, if any, & costs of disposal

3) Net amount reduces cost of primary product or joint costs

Capital Budgeting

Used to evaluate capital expenditures – uses 2 equations

    Cash inflows before tax
  – Depreciation on investment
  = Increase in taxable income
  – Tax
  = Increase in accounting net income

	Cash inflows before tax	**or**		Increase in accounting net income
–	Tax		+	Depreciation on investment
=	After tax net cash inflows		=	After tax net cash inflows

Payback Method

       Initial investment

÷   After tax net cash inflows

=   Payback period

Payback period is compared to target period

- If shorter, investment is acceptable
- If longer, investment is unacceptable

Accounting Rate of Return

   Increase in accounting net income
÷ Investment
= Accounting rate of return

Investment may be:
- Initial investment
- Long-term average - (initial investment + salvage value) ÷ 2
- Short-term average − (beginning carrying value + ending carrying value) ÷ 2

Return compared to target rate
- If greater, investment is acceptable
- If lower, investment is unacceptable

Internal Rate of Return

      Initial investment
÷   After tax net cash inflows
=   Present value factor (same as payback period)

Present value factor is compared to factors for same # of periods (life of investment) to determine effective interest rate

- Factor may be equal to amount at specific interest rate
- If factor falls between amounts, rate is estimated

Resulting rate compared to target rate

- If greater, investment is acceptable
- If lower, investment is unacceptable

Net Present Value

      After tax net cash inflows

X   Present value factor for annuity at target rate

=   Present value of investment

-    Initial investment

=   Net present value

If positive, investment is acceptable – If negative, investment is unacceptable

Special Analyses for Decision Making

Sensitivity analysis used to evaluate results of decisions under various conditions

May involve various techniques

Probability Analysis

Long-term average result (expected value) of decision is estimated

1) Each possible outcome of decision is assigned a probability

2) Total of probabilities is 100%

3) Profit or loss under each possible outcome is determined

4) Profit or loss for outcome multiplied by probability

5) Total of results is added

6) Result is long-term average result

Relevant Costing

Increase or decrease in profits or costs resulting from decision is analyzed

1) Determine increase or decrease in revenues that will result from decision

2) Determine increase or decrease in variable costs that will result from decision

3) Determine if decision will affect fixed costs

4) Net of change in revenues, variable costs, & fixed costs is relevant cost of making decision

Product & Service Pricing

Factors that affect price of product or service

- Cost of manufacturing & delivering product or cost of delivering service

- Quality of product or service

- Life of product

- Customers' preferences as to quality or price

Pricing Models

Profit based on sales price		Profit based on cost	
Sales price	100%	Sales price	100% + profit %
Cost	100% - profit %	Cost	100%
Gross profit	Profit %	Gross profit	Profit %

Governmental Accounting

Objective of governmental accounting & reporting – **accountability**

- Provide useful information
- Benefit wide range of users

Governmental financial information should:

- Demonstrate operations within legal restraints imposed by citizens
- Communication compliance with laws & regulations related to raising & spending public money
- Demonstrate **interperiod equity** – current period expenditures financed with current revenues

To demonstrate full accountability for all activities, information must include:

- Cost of services
- Sufficiency of revenues for services provided
- Financial position

Funds

Government comprised of funds – self-balancing sets of accounts – 3 categories
- Governmental
- Proprietary
- Fiduciary

Methods of Accounting

Funds of a governmental unit use two methods of accounting
- Most funds use **modified accrual accounting**
- Some funds use accrual accounting

Modified Accrual Accounting

Differs from accrual accounting:
- Focus of financial reporting is financial position & flow of resources
- Revenues are recognized when they become available & measurable
- Expenditures are recorded when goods or services are obtained
- Expenditures classified by **object, function, or character**

Financial Statements of Governmental Units

General purpose financial statements – referred to as **Comprehensive Annual Financial Report (CAFR)** – 5 components

- Management discussions & analysis – Required supplementary information presented before financial statements
- Government-wide financial statements
- Fund financial statements
- Notes to financial statements
- Required supplementary information

Users should be able to distinguish between primary government & component units – component units may be **blended** when either:

- Governing body of component is essentially the same as that of the primary government
- The component provides services almost exclusively for the primary government

Most component units will be **discretely presented**

Management Discussion & Analysis (MD & A)

Introduces basic financial statements & provides analytical overview of government's financial activities

Should include:

- Condensed comparison of current year financial information to prior year
- Analysis of overall financial position and results of operations
- Analysis of balances and transactions in individual funds
- Analysis of significant budget variance
- Description of capital assets and long-term debt activity during the period
- Currently known facts, decisions, or conditions expected to affect financial position or results of operations

Government-Wide Financial Statements

Consist of:

- Statement of Net Assets

- Statement of Activities

Report on overall government

- Do not display information about individual funds

- Exclude fiduciary activities or component units that are fiduciary

- Distinction made between primary government and discretely presented component units

- Distinction made between government activities and business-type activities of primary government

Characteristics of Government-Wide Financial Statements

Use economic measurement focus for all assets, liabilities, revenues, expenses, gains, & losses

Apply accrual basis of accounting

Revenues from exchanges or exchange-like transactions recognized in period of exchange

Revenues from non-exchange transactions:

- **Derived tax revenues** imposed on exchange transactions recognized as asset & revenues when exchange occurs
- **Imposed non-exchange revenues** imposed on non-government agencies recognized as asset when government has enforceable claim & as revenues when use of resources required or permitted
- **Government-mandated non-exchange transactions** provided by one level of government for another recognized as asset & revenue (or liability & expense) when all eligibility requirements met
- **Voluntary non-exchange transactions** recognized similarly to government-mandated non-exchange transactions

Statement of Net Assets

Presents assets & liabilities

- Assets & liabilities in order of liquidity

- Current & noncurrent portions of liabilities reported

- Assets – liabilities = Net assets

3 categories of net assets

- **Net assets invested in capital assets, net of related debt** – All capital assets, including restricted assets, net of depreciation & reduced by bonds, mortgages, notes, & other borrowings

- **Restricted net assets** – Assets with externally imposed restrictions on use distinguishing major categories of restrictions

- **Unrestricted net assets** – Remainder

Format of Statement of Net Assets

Assets, liabilities, & net assets reported for primary government

- Separate columns for governmental activities & business-type activities
- Amounts combined in total column

Assets, liabilities, & net assets also reported for component units

- Amounts reported similarly as those for primary government
- Column is **not** combined with totals for primary government

Statement of Activities

Self-financing activities distinguished from those drawing from general revenues

For each government function

- Net expense or revenue
- Relative burden

Governmental activities presented by function

Business-type activities presented by business segment

Items reported separately after net expenses of government's functions:

- General revenues
- Contributions to term & permanent endowments
- Contributions to permanent fund principal
- Special items – those that are unusual **or** infrequent
- Extraordinary items – those that are unusual **and** infrequent
- Transfers

Items on Statement of Activities

Depreciation – indirect expense charged to function with asset

- Allocated among functions for shared assets
- Not required to be allocated to functions for general capital assets
- Not allocated to functions for general infrastructure assets

Revenues classified into categories

- Amounts received from users or beneficiaries of a program always **program revenues**
- Amounts received from parties outside citizenry are **general revenues** if unrestricted or program revenues if restricted to specific programs
- Amounts received from taxpayers always general revenues
- Amounts generated by the government usually general revenues
- Contributions to term & permanent endowments, contributions to permanent fund principal, special & extraordinary items, & transfers reported separately

Format of Statement of Activities

Information for each program or function reported separately:

- Expenses
- Charges for services
- Operating grants & contributions
- Capital grants & contributions

Difference between expenses & revenues reported for each program

- Equal to change in net assets
- Separated into columns for governmental activities and business-type activities
- Combined into a total column

Remaining items (general revenues, grants & contributions, special & extraordinary items, & transfers) reported separately below functions & programs

- Divided into governmental activities & business-type activities with total column
- Provides change in net assets & ending net assets with same amounts as Statement of net assets
- Separate column for component units not combined into total

Additional Characteristics of Government-Wide Financial Statements

Internal Amounts

- Eliminated to avoid doubling up
- Interfund receivables & payables eliminated
- Amounts due between governmental & business-type activities presented as offsetting internal balances

Capital assets include the following:

- Land, land improvements, & easements
- Buildings & building improvements
- Vehicles, machinery, & equipment
- Works of art & historical treasures
- Infrastructure
- All other tangible & intangible assets with initial useful lives > a single period

Accounting for Capital Assets & Infrastructure

Capital assets reported at historical cost

- Includes capitalized interest & costs of getting asset ready for intended use
- Depreciated over useful lives
- Inexhaustible assets not depreciated
- Infrastructure assets may be depreciated under modified approach

Infrastructure includes:

- Capital assets with longer lives than most capital assets that are normally stationary
- Roads, bridges, tunnels, drainage systems, water & sewer systems, dams, & lighting systems

Eligible infrastructure assets not depreciated

- Must be part of network or subsystem maintained & preserved at established condition levels
- Additions & improvements increasing capacity or efficiency capitalized
- Other expenditures expensed

Fund Financial Statements

Separate financial statements prepared for governmental, proprietary, & fiduciary funds

Governmental funds include:

- General fund
- Special revenue funds
- Capital projects funds
- Debt service funds
- Permanent funds

Proprietary funds include:

- Enterprise funds
- Internal service funds

Fiduciary funds include"

- Pension & other employee benefit trust funds
- Investment trust funds
- Private purpose trust funds
- Agency funds

Financial Statements of Governmental Funds

Statements of governmental funds

- Balance sheet
- Statement of revenues, expenditures, and changes in fund balances

Focus is to report sources, uses, & balances of current financial resources

- Apply modified accrual accounting
- Capital assets & long-term debt not reported as assets or liabilities

Balance Sheet

Reports assets, liabilities, & fund balances

- Reported separately for each major governmental fund
- Fund balances segregated into reserved & unreserved

Total fund balances reconciled to net assets of governmental activities in government-wide financial statements

Statement of Revenues, Expenditures, & Changes in Fund Balances

Reports inflows, outflows, and balances of current financial resources
- Reported separately for each major governmental fund
- Revenues classified by major source
- Expenditures classified by function

Format of statement:

Revenues
- Expenditures
= Excess (deficiency) of revenues over expenditures
± Other financing sources and uses
± Special and extraordinary items
= Net change in fund balances
+ Fund balances – beginning of period
= Fund balances – end of period

Change in fund balances reconciled to change in net assets of governmental activities in government-wide financial statements

Financial Statements of Proprietary Funds

Statements of proprietary funds

- Statement of net assets
- Statement of Revenues, Expenses, and Changes in Fund Net Assets
- Statement of Cash Flows

Preparation of statements

- Emphasis is measurement of economic resources
- Prepared under accrual basis of accounting

Statement of Net Assets

Prepared in classified format

- Current & noncurrent assets & liabilities distinguished
- Net assets reported in same categories as used in government-wide financial statements

Statement of Revenues, Expenses, & Changes in Fund Net Assets

Amounts should be the same as net assets & changes in net assets shown for business-type activities in government-wide financial statements
- Revenues reported by major source
- Operating & nonoperating revenues & expenses distinguished
- Nonoperating revenues & expenses reported after operating income

Format of statement of revenues, expenses, & changes in fund net assets

Operating revenues (listed by source)

-    Operating expenses (listed by category)

=   Operating income or loss

±   Nonoperating revenues & expenses

=   Income before other revenues, expenses, gains, losses, & transfers

±   Capital contributions, additions to permanent & term endowments, special & extraordinary items, & transfers

=   Increase or decrease in net assets

+ Net assets – beginning of period

=   Net assets – end of period

Statement of Cash Flows

Shows sources & uses of cash by major classification

- Operating activities reported using direct method
- Noncapital financing activities
- Capital & related financing activities
- Investing activities

Operating income reconciled to cash flows from operating activities (indirect method)

Financial Statements of Fiduciary Funds

Statements of fiduciary funds

- Statement of Net Assets
- Statement of Changes in Fiduciary Net Assets

Focus of fiduciary financial statements

- Emphasis on measurement of economic resources
- Prepared using accrual basis of accounting

Notes to Financial Statements

Intended to provide information needed for fair presentation of financial statements

Notes will include:

- Summary of significant accounting policies
- Disclosure about capital assets & long-term liabilities
- Disclosure about major classes of capital assets
- Disclosure about donor-restricted endowments
- Segment information

Required Supplementary Information

Presented in addition to MD & A

Consists of:

- Budgetary comparison schedules for governmental funds
- Information about infrastructure reported under the modified approach

Governmental Funds

A governmental unit maintains 5 types of governmental funds

- General fund – all activities not accounted for in another fund

- Special revenue funds – account for revenues earmarked to finance specific activities

- Capital projects funds – account for construction of fixed assets

- Debt service fund – accumulates resources for payment of general obligation debts of other governmental funds

- Permanent funds – account for resources that are legally restricted

Assets & liabilities of governmental funds are maintained in account groups

- **General fixed assets account group** – accounts for fixed assets of governmental funds

- **General long-term debt account group** – accounts for principal portion of obligations paid through debt service funds

General Fund Accounting

A governmental unit will have one general fund

- Annual budget is recorded at the beginning of the year
- Revenues, expenditure, & other financing sources & uses are recorded during the year
- Adjustments are made at the balance sheet date
- Budgetary accounts are closed at year-end

Beginning of Year

Governmental unit adopts annual budget for general fund

Budget recorded with following entry:

Estimated revenues control	XXX	
Estimated other financing sources	XXX	
Budgetary fund balance	XXX or	XXX
Appropriations		XXX
Estimated other financing uses		XXX

Estimated revenues control = revenues expected to be collected during the year

Estimated other financing sources = estimate of proceeds from bond issues & operating transfers in

Budgetary fund balance = plug – amount required to balance the entry

Appropriations = expenditures expected during the year

Estimated other financing uses = expected operating transfers out

During the Year

Revenue cycle consists of billing certain revenues, such as property taxes, collecting billed revenues, writing off uncollectible billings, & collecting unbilled revenues

Billing of revenues:

Taxes receivable	XXX	
Allowance for estimated uncollectible taxes		XXX
Deferred revenues		XXX
Revenues control		XXX

Taxes receivable = amount billed

Allowance for estimated uncollectible taxes = billings expected to be uncollectible

- This amount may be adjusted upward or downward during the year
- Offsetting entry will be to revenues control

Deferred revenues = portion of billed taxes expected to be collected more than 60 days after close of current year

Revenues control = portion of billed taxes expected to be collected during the current year or within 60 days of close

During the Year (continued)

Collecting billed revenues:

Cash	XXX	
Taxes receivable		XXX

Writing off uncollectible amounts:

Allowance for estimated uncollectible taxes	XXX	
Taxes receivable		XXX

Collecting unbilled revenues:

Cash	XXX	
Revenues control		XXX

During the Year (continued)

Spending cycle consists of ordering goods & services, receiving the goods & services, and paying for them

Ordering goods & services:

Encumbrances control (estimated cost)	XXX	
Budgetary fund balance reserved for encumbrances		XXX

Receiving goods & services:

Budgetary fund balance reserved for encumbrances (estimated cost)	XXX	
Encumbrances control		XXX
Expenditures control (actual cost)	XXX	
Vouchers payable		XXX

Payment:

Vouchers payable	XXX	
Cash		XXX

During the Year (continued)

Other financing sources & uses are recorded as the transactions occur:

- Bond proceeds are recorded as other financing sources when received

- Operating transfers to or from other funds are reported as other financing uses or sources as the funds are transferred

Adjustments at Balance Sheet Date

Closing entry – eliminating revenues, expenditures, & encumbrances:

Revenues control	XXX	
Unreserved fund balance (plug)	XXX or	XXX
Expenditures control		XXX
Encumbrances control		XXX

The remaining balance in the budgetary fund balance reserved for encumbrances is transferred to a nonbudgetary account:

Budgetary fund balance reserved for encumbrances	XXX	
Fund balance reserved for encumbrances		XXX

The governmental unit may decide to recognize inventory as an asset:

Inventories (increase)	XXX	
Fund balance reserved for inventories		XXX

or

Fund balance reserved for inventories	XXX	
Inventories (decrease)		XXX

End of Year

Budget recorded in beginning of year is reversed:

Appropriations	XXX		
Estimated other financing uses	XXX		
Budgetary fund balance	XXX	or	XXX
Estimated revenues control			XXX
Estimated other financing sources			XXX

Special Revenue Fund

Used to account for revenues that must be used for a particular purpose

- Does not include expendable trusts or capital projects
- Accounting identical to general fund

Capital Projects Fund

Used to account for construction of fixed assets

- Fund opened when project commences & closed when project complete
- Accounting similar to general fund

Differences in accounting for capital projects fund:

1) Budgetary entries generally not made
2) Expenditures generally made under contract
   - Credit contracts payable
   - Credit retention payable for deferred payments

Debt Service Fund

Used to account for funds accumulated to make principal & interest payments on general obligation debts

- Expenditures include principal & interest payable in current period

- Resources consist of amounts transferred from other funds (other financing sources) & earnings on investments (revenues)

Amounts used for interest payments separated from amounts used for principal payments

Cash for interest	XXX	
Cash for principal	XXX	
Other financing sources		XXX

General Fixed Asset Account Group

Used to account for assets acquired or constructed by governmental unit
- Includes assets acquired through general fund, special revenue fund, or capital projects fund
- Assets acquired through accrual funds accounted for in that fund

General fixed assets:
- Includes land, buildings, equipment, & automobiles
- Also includes construction in progress from capital projects fund
- May include infrastructure such as streets & sidewalks

As assets are acquired or constructed:
- Acquiring fund will record as expenditure
- General fixed asset account group records the asset

Asset (identifying appropriate category)   XXX
   Investment in general fixed assets
     from (identify source)   XXX

General Fixed Asset Account Group (continued)

Assets received by donation are recorded at fair value

Governmental unit may elect to account for depreciation:

Investment in general fixed assets from (identify source)	XXX	
Accumulated depreciation		XXX

Disposals of general fixed assets result in revenues in fund receiving money – general fixed asset account group records:

Investment in general fixed assets from (identify source)	XXX	
Asset		XXX

General Long-Term Debt Account Group

Used to account for principal portion of long-term debt to be repaid out of general revenues

- Not used to account for debts of proprietary or fiduciary funds
- Not used to account for short-term debt

Issuance of debt results in entries in fund receiving proceeds & general long-term debt account group

Receiving fund:

Cash	XXX	
Other financing sources control		XXX

General long-term debt account group:

Amount to be provided for retirement of debt	XXX	
Bonds payable		XXX

General Long-Term Debt Account Group (continued)

A premium is transferred to the debt service fund for the repayment of the bond

Transferring fund:

Other financing uses control	XXX	
Cash		XXX

Debt service fund:

Cash for principal	XXX	
Other financing sources control		XXX

General long-term debt account group:

Amount available in debt service fund	XXX	
Amount to be provided for retirement of debt		XXX

General Long-Term Debt Account Group (continued)

Upon maturity of debt, entries are made in the debt service fund & the general long-term debt account group:

Debt service fund:

Expenditures control	XXX	
Matured bonds payable		XXX
Matured bonds payable	XXX	
Cash for principal		XXX

General long-term debt account group:

Bonds payable	XXX	
Amount available in debt service fund		XXX

Proprietary Funds

Account for governmental activities conducted similarly to business enterprises

Enterprise fund:

- Used to account for business-type activities
- Uses accrual basis accounting
- Earned income recognized as operating revenues
- Shared taxes reported as nonoperating revenues

Internal service fund:

- Used to account for services provided to other governmental departments on a fee or cost-reimbursement basis
- Resources come from billings to other funds
- Reported as operating revenues

Fiduciary Funds

Pension Trust Fund

Accounts for contributions made by government & employees using accrual accounting

Additional information in notes and supplementary information following notes will include:

- Description of plan and classes of employees covered

- Summary of significant accounting policies

- Information about contributions including description of how contributions are determined and required contribution rates of plan members

- Information about legally required reserves at reporting date

Expendable Trust Fund

Accounts for assets put into trust where principal & income can be spent

- Uses modified accrual accounting
- Resources used in accordance with purpose of fund

Agency Fund

Accounts for money collected for various funds, other governments, or outsiders

- Includes only balance sheet accounts
- Assets always equal liabilities

Interfund Transactions

Operating transfers are transfers of resources from one fund to another such as a transfer of money from the general fund to a capital projects fund

Paying fund:
Other financing uses control	XXX	
Cash		XXX

Receiving fund:
Cash	XXX	
Other financing sources control		XXX

Residual equity transfers are transfers of resources to establish a special purpose fund or to close the fund when the purpose has been completed

Paying fund:
Unreserved fund balance	XXX	
Cash		XXX

Receiving fund:
Cash	XXX	
Unreserved fund balance **or** Contributed capital		XXX

Interfund Transactions (continued)

Quasi-external transactions occur when one fund acquires goods or services from another in a transaction similar to one that would occur with outsiders

Paying fund:
    Expenditures control **or** Expenses   XXX
        Cash   XXX

Receiving fund:
    Cash   XXX
        Revenues control   XXX

Reimbursements occur when one fund makes payments on behalf of another fund

Reimbursing fund:
    Expenditures control **or** Expenses   XXX
        Cash   XXX

Receiving fund:
    Cash   XXX
        Expenditures control **or** Expenses   XXX

Interfund Transactions (continued)

Loans may be made one fund to another

Lending fund:
    Due from other fund (fund identified)   XXX
        Cash   XXX

Receiving fund:
    Cash   XXX
        Due to other fund (fund identified)   XXX

Capital Leases

When governmental fund enters into capital lease, 3 funds affected:

Fund entering lease:

Expenditures control (present value)	XXX	
Other financing sources control		XXX

General fixed asset account group:

Asset (identifying appropriate category)	XXX	
Investment in general fixed assets		
from capital leases		XXX

General long-term debt account group:

Amount to be provided for lease payments	XXX	
Capital leases payable		XXX

Solid Waste Landfill Operations

Environmental Protection Agency imposes requirements on governments operating waste landfills

- Procedures for closures

- Procedures for post-closure care

Procedures represent long-term obligations accounted for as long-term debt

- Costs to be incurred by governmental funds accounted for in general long-term debt account group

- Expenditures in governmental funds reduce general long-term debt account group balances

- Costs to be incurred by proprietary funds accounted for directly in funds

- Costs associated with closure and post-closure procedures accounted for during periods of operation

Accounting for Nonprofit Entities

Financial Statements of Not-for-Profit Organizations

All not-for-profit organizations must prepare at least 3 financial statements

Not-for-profit organizations include:

- Hospitals
- Colleges & universities
- Voluntary health & welfare organizations (VHW)

Required financial statements for all types include:

- Statement of Financial Position
- Statement of Activities
- Statement of Cash Flows

VHWs must also prepare a Statement of Functional Expenses

Statement of Financial Position

Includes assets, liabilities, & net assets

- Unrestricted net assets – available for general use, including those set aside by board of trustees
- Temporarily restricted net assets – donated by outside party & restricted to specific purpose
- Permanently restricted net assets – donated by outside party & required to be invested with earnings restricted or unrestricted

Statement of Financial Position (continued)

Not-for-Profit Company
Statement of Financial Position
December 31, 19X2

Assets:		Liabilities:	
Cash	100	Accounts payable	50
Marketable securities	300	Notes payable	100
Accounts receivable, net	40	Bonds payable	100
Inventory	120	Total liabilities	250
P, P, & E	80	Net assets:	
Total assets	640	Unrestricted	45
		Temporarily restricted	305
		Permanently restricted	40
		Total net assets	390
		Total liabilities & net assets	640

Statement of Activities

Similar to income statement

- Reports revenues, gains, expenses, & losses

- Also reports temporarily restricted assets released from restriction

- Categorized activities among unrestricted, temporarily restricted, & permanently restricted to provide change in net assets for each

- Change added to beginning balance to provide ending net assets for each category

Expenses classified by:

- Object - nature of item or service obtained

- Function - program or activity to which attributed

- Character - period or periods benefited from payments

Statement of Activities (continued)

Not-for-Profit Company
Statement of Activities
For Year Ended December 31, 19X2

	Total	Unrestricted	Temporarily Restricted	Permanently Restricted
Revenues & gains				
Donations	665	265	360	40
Investment income	10	10		
Total revenues & gains	675	275	360	40
Net assets released				
from restriction				
Research restrictions		100	(100)	
Time restrictions				
Property restrictions		20	(20)	
Total net assets released				
from restriction		120	(120)	
Expenses & losses				
Depreciation	(10)	(10)		
Program expenses	(190)	(190)		
General & administrative	(85)	(85)		
Salaries	(70)	(70)		
Total expenses & losses	(355)	(355)		
Change in net assets	320	40	240	40
Net assets at December 31, 19X1	70	5	65	
Net assets at December 31, 19X2	390	45	305	40

Statement of Cash Flows

Similar to statement of cash flows under GAAP

- Special treatment for donated assets restricted for long-term purposes
- Classified as cash flows from financing activities

Statement of Functional Expenses

Classifies expenses into program services & support services

- Program services – expenses directly related to organization's purpose
- Support services – expenses necessary, but not directly related to organization's purpose such as fund raising & administrative expenses

Expenses classified by (similar to statement of activities):

- Object
- Nature
- Character

Contributions Made to and Received by Not-for-Profit Organizations

In general, contributions are income to a not-for-profit organization

- Those that are part of the major, ongoing, & central operations are revenues
- Those that are not are gains

Unrestricted cash donations:

Cash	XXX	
Donations (unrestricted funds)		XXX

Permanently restricted donations:

Cash	XXX	
Donations (permanently restricted funds)		XXX

Donated services:

Program expense (fair market value)	XXX	
Donations (unrestricted funds)		XXX

Contributions Made to and Received by Not-for-Profit Organizations (continued)

Cash donations restricted for a specific purposes:

When made:

Cash	XXX	
Donations (temporarily restricted funds)		XXX

When used:

Temporarily restricted net assets	XXX	
Unrestricted net assets		XXX
Expense	XXX	
Cash		XXX

Cash donated for purchase of property:

When made:

Cash	XXX	
Donations (temporarily restricted funds)		XXX

When used:

Temporarily restricted net assets	XXX	
Unrestricted net assets		XXX
Property	XXX	
Cash		XXX

Pledges

Promises by outside parties to donate assets

- Recognized in period of pledge

- Allowance for uncollectible amount established

- Some or all may have time restriction – temporarily restricted

- Some or all may be unrestricted

Pledges	XXX	
Allowance for uncollectible pledges		XXX
Donations (unrestricted funds)		XXX
Donations (temporarily restricted funds)		XXX

Other Donations

Donations of art, antiques, or artifacts not recognized if:

- Asset held for research or exhibition
- Asset preserved & unaltered
- Proceeds from sale of asset to be used to buy additional art, antiques, & artifacts

Donated assets to be held in trust

- Not recognized by not-for-profit organization
- Disclosed in footnotes to financial statements

Hospital Revenues

Patient service revenue recorded at gross value of services

- Billing may be less due to Medicare allowance or employee discount

- Difference recorded in allowance account

- Statement of activities will report net amount

Services provided for free due to charity not recognized as revenues

Special transactions:

- Bad debts recognized as expense on statement of activities, not reduction of revenues

- Miscellaneous revenues from cafeteria, gift shop, parking lot fees, & educational programs classified as other revenue

- Donated supplies reported as operating revenue & expense when used

- Donations of essential services and unrestricted donations are nonoperating revenues

College Tuition Revenues

Students may receive refunds or price breaks

Refunds to students reduce tuition revenues

Price breaks may result from scholarships or reductions for family members of faculty or staff

- Tuition recognized at gross amount
- Price break recognized as expense

Index

Index

213

Index

Index

Index

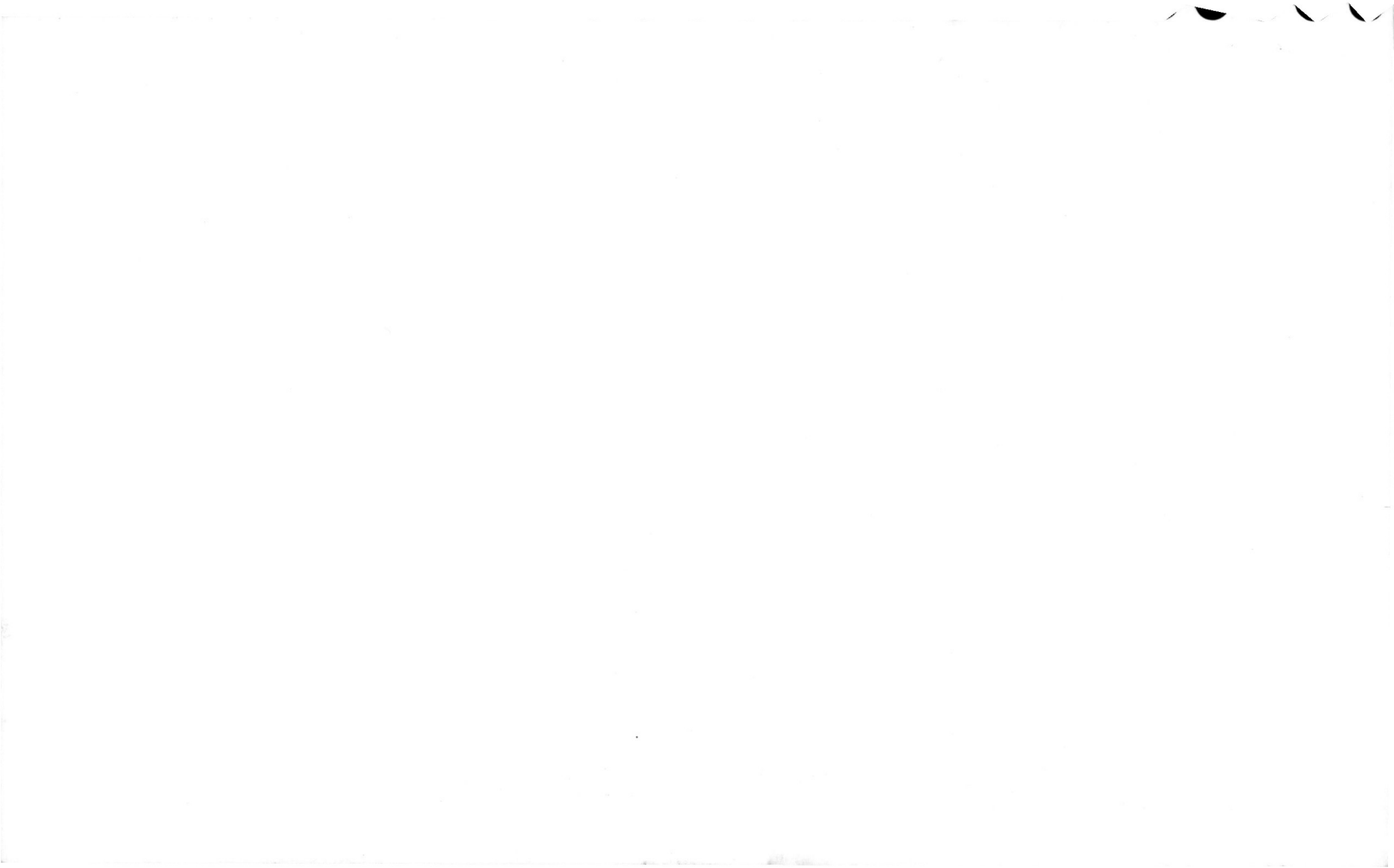